The Fundamentals of Finances Applied to Everyday Living

Robin R. Haynes

Larry –
Thank you for
your support.
Continued Success
Robin
2013

The Fundamentals of Finances Applied to Everyday Living

ISBN 978-0-578-115160

Library of Congress Control Number: 2013930289

Credits:
Cover Design: Mad Graphics
Editors: Patricia A. Rhodes & Dr. Hope E. Rhodes-Pretlow
Publisher: Everyday Publishing Group LLC
Foreword: Carmen M. Stone-Roberts
Photography: Jazzy Studio Photography

This book is dedicated to my son Ryan Jr. and, my two nieces Eden, and Jordan; you three are the reason why I do what I do! Mommy and Auntie Robin loves you totally.

I truly thank GOD for the three of you!!!

Acknowledgments

First giving honor to GOD and GOD alone for giving me such an awesome gift. To my husband Ryan Sr., thank you for taking this ride with me. To my parents, Robert Sr. and, Patricia, your love and support is what has sustained me during my not so smooth times. My siblings Robert Jr. and Hope, where do I begin? Thank you for your continuous encouragement and support! I love you both from the bottom of my heart you know this! My grandmothers, Mrs. Bertie Rhodes-Gibson, and Mrs. Annie M. Williams, thank you for laying a solid foundation for us. My family, both near and extended, you have played a major role in my life whether you know it or not. THANK YOU, I love you dearly. Jay and Yolanda, the Founder, and Co-Founder of Everyday Publishing Group, thank you for allowing me this opportunity to use this form of communication of getting the message out. Aisha and the Jazzy Photos team, thank you for making me beautiful - LOL. Quinn, Shawn, Janae, Ms. Cheryl, and Demitra THANK YOU for allowing me to bounce this book off of you. To Dr. Phyllis Keys, (no matter what you will always be Dr. Keys to me), thank you for your ear as well as your advice, I am truly grateful. To Carmen, Jerry and, Lisa thank you for being the friends that you are. Your friendships are very dear to me, and our conversations are the best. To those folks who have stuck by me from then to now thank you, you know who you are.

Finally, to all of my readers, my fans, my students, and those persons who I have touched with my teachings, thank you for allowing me every opportunity to speak to you. It gives me great joy to be able to teach and talk to you all about understanding your finances and helping you reach your financial goals. Thank you for your continuous support! I love you all.

Foreword

By Carmen M. Stone Roberts

How many of us are able to live out our dreams and desires??

Following your dreams is exactly what my friend, Robin, did!! ---She would tell me throughout my life, "Carmen, it is imperative to 'take leaps of faith' in order to gain success at any level".

When I met Robin in 2000, I met a young woman that loved the Lord and anyone that crossed her path knew that she always put him FIRST. Her demeanor was and still is very magnetic and captivating.

For many years, Robin and I worked together in the financial industry and, as I grew to know her, I had a lot of admiration for her drive, tenacity and strong work ethics. She portrayed passion beyond measure to teach and educate her clients. Robin and I shared an overwhelming desire to assist clients, especially in our community, about financial literacy. We would often chat about how we loved our careers and would challenge ourselves to reach out to as many people as we could.

Her willingness to proclaim the benefits of managing your finances allowed her to grow and do some major balancing in her own life. With being a wife and mother, she had the tools to always sustain her family. Being along with Robin in this journey, she is truly a woman of her word and embraces all of what life has to offer.

Robin always concentrated on what mattered most to her and her family. With having God's infinite wisdom on her side, she set definite goals in her life and achieved all that her heart desired. In "Fundamentals of Finances Applied to Everyday Living", she will encourage you to aim high, do what you love and keep an open mind. This book will mark the beginning of your individual journey and financial wellness.

It has truly been a blessing to know my friend and to watch her grow as an Author, CEO and Founder.

Be encouraged in what she has to share with us and always follow your instincts and cherish what life has to offer you.

Peace and blessings...All my love, your friend and Sister in Christ.

Table of Contents

Introduction

"Do what you can, with what you have, where you are."
— **Theodore Roosevelt – 26th U.S. President**

The financial world can be extremely complicated and frustrating for the average consumer. Honestly before I started working in the financial industry, I really had no idea how intense this world was. Terms such as CD (certificate of deposit), money market accounts, APR (annual percentage rate) were things I never understood. When people would say, "I am going to open a CD," I honestly thought they were referring to a music CD. I had no clue what language was being spoken. It's funny, I recall getting my first savings account and ATM card. I thought I had arrived. I was going to the ATM machine to withdraw my money; I knew I was officially on the financial scene and no one could tell me anything. Needless to say after I was hired as a teller years ago, my thought process completely changed. It was at that point that I realized that the financial world was much bigger than a savings account and an ATM card.

Having been in the financial industry for over a decade, it is my belief that people do not have a complete understanding of their finances and how they work. Therefore, there is a need to teach the basics of finances.

Not only do these concepts need to be taught, they need to be broken down so that they are clear and easy to understand.

As you begin to read this part of The Fundamentals of Finances series, there will be some terms, concepts, and ideas that are familiar, and you may ask yourself, "Who doesn't know this?" Believe it or not, while these concepts may seem simple to you, there are still 75-80% of people who are unfamiliar with these basic financial concepts. In this part of the series, we will not cause you to have brain overload; however we will discuss basic ideas and concepts that will help you understand your money and your overall financial picture. We will also discuss steps to help you prepare your financial goal(s) which is the foundation of becoming and sustaining financial success. As you continue to read I encourage you to highlight, write down and revisit concepts that may seem unclear. Before we begin, please take a moment to answer the following financial questions. We will revisit these questions along our journey.

What are your strongest financial areas?

_____

What are your weakest financial areas?

_____

What do you fear the most about your finances?

_____

Having An Impact

"No one knows for certain how much impact they have on the lives of other people. Oftentimes, we have no clue. Yet we push it just the same."
— Jay Asher – Author

After working in a financial organization for over a decade, I never knew how much of an impact I would have on people's financial well-being. Two years into my position as a teller, I knew I wanted to continue to assist clients with understanding their finances. I am always in awe of how many people do not understand their personal finances. I am not talking about stocks, bonds and annuities. I am referring to the basic stuff, such as knowing the difference between a savings and checking account, and knowing what financial institution best fits your financial needs.

I can recall in my early years as a teller, how everyone was extremely happy to cash their check on payday. I witnessed clients visiting the closest branch to do a withdrawal of everything that had been deposited into their accounts on payday. I would always ask myself – why aren't they saving? Why does someone need to walk around with $800.00 in their pocket? After six months of being a teller, and having studied the various products and services that the institution offered, I started having conversations to encourage the "check cashers." I would advise them to open a checking account or to save at least $20.00 a pay for a rainy day. I would discuss the various savings, checking, and money market accounts available, focusing on how great the interest rates were. Back then the interest rates were approximately 4.00% on a basic savings account, 2.75% on a checking account, and 11.00% on a certificate of deposit. They were really good rates - those were the days. After having various conversations, my "check cashers" really took heed to what I said. I noticed that they developed an interest in opening accounts and saving for that rainy day. It was at this point that I noticed on payday, there were clients waiting in line just for me. They started to request more information. They wanted to know the latest interest rates on various accounts. They also asked basic questions about their existing accounts. And they inquired about additional ways to save. I gained a reputation as the "favorite teller". Simply by asking a few basic questions and encouraging clients to give routine consideration to their financial well-being, clients started a process of understanding their finances. It is my hope to take you through a similar journey.

After leaving the teller line, I became a processor for both loans and new accounts. WOW, now talk about having to learn a lot. I had to process or open new accounts, input and disperse loans. This was a lot to learn and understand. Having become baptized in the financial water, by making the transition from the teller line to becoming a processor, forced my knowledge of the financial world to blossom. I wanted to learn everything there was to learn about the financial industry. Being a processor was more than a job to me. No matter what my client's financial picture looked like, I knew that I could help them in some capacity. I would take the time to build a relationship with every client that I had a chance to speak with. A bond of trust was at the foundation of each of those relationships. I was taught to treat every client like a family member, and that is what I began to do. Every client was a part of my financial family. If I went on vacation, my clients would get upset. As I reflect, I really had an impact.

I never knew how much of an impact I had while working in finances. I can recall one memorable situation:

While sitting in my office, my client and I started discussing her various financial goals. She informed me that banking was new to her, and that she really did not have an idea of what to do. After hearing and listening to what the client was saying, I then started to go over various ways to help her achieve her financial goals. She wanted to return to school, however she always had an issue with math. I gave her one of my motivational speeches, on how she could do anything she set her mind to. Needless to say, at the end of our session we were both in tears. This is the end of the conversation:

Client: "Thank you Ms. Robin for everything"

Me: "No problem, glad I could help you"

Client: Through tears "Ms. Robin, you don't understand, all of my life, people looked down on me because, I never knew certain things, like not knowing what to do with my money. People told me that I was wasting my time going back to school, because I didn't know math, and because of this I was really frustrated. Not only did you take your time to explain to me what the various accounts were, you believed in me enough to tell me that I can do anything I put my mind too."

As my client kept talking, tears started to form in my eyes. It was at this moment that I knew I had to assist everyone that crossed my path with their finances. No matter how small or how big their financial situation, I had to assist them. Often times I would get asked by my management team whether I was paying my clients or even my colleagues to write or say nice things about me. Having been asked this question a million times, I would simply say, "Nope, I just love what I do, and I care about the financial well-being of my clients." The management team seemed astonished because I actually cared, and it showed.

I shared that story with you so that you can understand that my goal is to help you in becoming financially
successful. I know that having lack of money or not
having a good credit score can deter you from achieving
this success. But here is the key, you have to put certain
tools into play that can and will help you as you travel
your financial journey. Will it be easy? *NO*. Can you do
it? *YES*. I encourage you as you begin to read this part
of the series, to focus on your areas of financial weakness.
You may say, "I am weak in all financial areas, I don't
know where to begin." I know that after reading this
book, those things which seemed unclear, will become
clear. If you are reading this book, your journey of
becoming financially successful is underway.

It Takes Preparation

"I know God won't give me anything I can't handle. I just
wish he didn't trust me so much."
— **Mother Teresa**

Before you attempt to understand your finances or
reconstruct your financial picture, you must first prepare
yourself spiritual, mentally, emotionally, and physically.
Understanding your finances is almost like learning to
ride a bicycle. You have to have the mindset to take
preventative measures that will keep you from falling. If
you happen to fall, know that you will be OK. You have
the ability to try again.

I recall as a financial consultant when my established
clients expressed interest in opening additional accounts
to save money for major purchases (house, car, vacation,
etc.). I would ask them to consider the following: What
type of new account(s) are you looking to open? How
much money do you plan to save? What is the timeframe
to accomplish this goal? The majority of these clients had
not given consideration to these questions. I share this
with you, so you understand this process requires time,
patience, and preparation.

Facing change can be difficult. Being on the threshold of change does require some type of *spiritual guidance*. I have learned throughout life, that seeking help from GOD can provide ease in everything that you do, including getting a better understanding of your finances. **"God will meet all your needs according to His glorious riches in Christ Jesus."** Philippians 4:19 (NIV)

I remember my clients and I had several conversations about the goodness of GOD. Yes, we at times had church in my office. My clients and I would discuss how GOD alone carried us through situations. We literally turned my office into a sanctuary. You are probably asking yourself, how does this relate to understanding your financial picture or becoming financially successful? I will tell you this; having a relationship with GOD will ease your fears and frustrations especially when it comes to your finances. Having a relationship with GOD will also help guide you along as you continue to travel throughout life.

The second key component as you prepare yourself to change your financial situation is *changing your mindset*. Changing the way you think can become a tedious task. We both know that when we have been doing certain things the same way for so long, we become comfortable and complacent. When do we change our way of thinking? When do we decide to become better in our everyday lives, including our eating habits and financial behaviors? The answer to this question lies within. You have to have the mindset to become better at understanding your financial picture along with doing better managing your finances. Once you have the mindset of overcoming your financial fears and challenges, the battle is half over.

During initial consultations with clients, the first thing I inform them is the need to understand their overall financial picture. I also encourage them to have the mindset that they can and will actually understand it. I can recall having a meeting with a young lady, and the first thing she said to me was, "I really don't understand this, I tried to understand, but I just don't get it."

My response was, "What is it that you don't get, is it that you become confused with what comes in (income) versus what goes out (expenses)?"

"Yes," she said. "That's it; I can't for the life of me understand why the numbers don't match" (monthly income versus monthly expenses). It was at this point that I requested a record of all monthly income, along with all monthly expenses. These are the itmes needed to analyze a budget. When reviewing the information, I noticed that she was not preparing herself mentally when paying her monthly expenses. How do you mentally prepare yourself to pay your bills? It's simple. For starters you need to know the **what**, and the **when** of each expense.

The most common expenses are as follows:
- Living Expenses (Mortgage or Rent)
- Utilities
- Cable/Internet
- Car payment and auto insurance
- Food (Grocery not fast food)
- Life insurance
- Health insurance

In order to prevent you from becoming overly frustrated, you have to know what expenses are to be paid and when they are to be paid. I suggest you start to mentally prepare yourself to pay these expenses around the 25th of the month prior to when they are due. For example, start preparing on January 25th to pay February's expenses. By doing this, when the first of the month rolls around, you will already have an established mindset to pay these expenses.

The third component in preparing to understand your finances is to recognize how *emotions* affect your finances. Finances and emotions are usually not compatible. Are you the type of person who spends when you are upset, happy, feeling unappreciated or lonely? Understanding your finances requires you have to have a clear head. Take time to recognize those things that cause you to overspend. Then, take steps to safeguard your finances when you are experiencing the aforementioned emotions.

The final component when it comes to preparing to revamp your financial picture is ***physically*** putting new financial behaviors into practice. We have covered the spiritual, mental, and emotional components. We now have to chat about changing behaviors. In order to become financially successful, you have to change your financial behaviors. For starters you have to stop feeling compelled to spend money. Especially money that you don't have. Often times we get in our own way. We sabotage our success, especially when it comes to our finances. This actually goes back to changing your MINDSET.

When I review client's short term and long term financial goals, I always advise them that the only way to reach their goals is to first change their thought process and then change their behaviors. I recall a client who was in the process of changing jobs. They said, "This is hard, I want to leave my job and find a job that I enjoy doing. But I don't have the financial resources to leave just yet." My response was "In everything that you do, you have to prepare. Set a goal and time frame to accomplish that goal." That is how you have to look at understanding your finances. You have to set a goal, and then allocate time, patience and effort for accomplishing that goal. We will talk about setting goals in Chapter 10.

Key Points:
1. Spiritual preparation: Having a relationship with GOD will ease your fears and frustrations
2. Mental preparation: Change your mindset
3. Emotional preparation: Be aware of how your emotions affect your finances.
4. Physical preparation: Set realistic goals and a realistic time frame to accomplish these goals.

Exercising Your Brain Power

In this chapter we have discussed that understanding your financial picture takes preparation from 4 angles.

Question A

What are the four areas of preparation needed to better understand your financial picture?

1) _____

2) _____

3) _____

4) _____

Question B

List 3 things for each aspect that you have listed in Question A to help you as you travel along your financial journey.

1) _____

   A) _____

     _____

   B) _____

     _____

   C) _____

     _____

2) _____

     _____

     _____

   A) _____

     _____

Robin R. Haynes
Educator/Author/Radio Host

t.443.632.7312
info@understandingfinances.org
www.understandingfinances.org

Understanding
FINANCES
Making Finances Easy

B) _____

_____

C) _____

_____

3) _____

A) _____

_____

B) _____

_____

C) _____

_____

4) _____

A) _____

_____

B) _____

_____

C) _____

_____

Knowing Where To Start

"You can't stop the future
You can't rewind the past
The only way to learn the secret
...is to press play."
— **Jay Asher – Author**

Not knowing where to start or how to start tackling your finances can be nerve racking. Now that we know that it takes preparation from every angle (spiritually, mentally, emotionally, and physically), it's now time for you to start chipping away at understanding your financial picture. So where do you begin? At what point do you start? It's simple, you start from the very beginning. Understanding your finances is like going to grade school, once you have completed elementary school; you are then ready for middle school. Knowing your path to becoming financially successful is just like progressing to the next grade level. You have to know the basics before you can advance.

Knowing what institution best fits your financial needs is a major piece of the puzzle that will help you become financially successful. How will you know what steps to take in becoming a financial success if you don't know what financial institution is best equipped to suite your needs? There are two financial institutions that are commonly known amongst most consumers, they are a commercial bank and a credit union. Believe it or not there are differences between the two. What are the differences? I am glad you asked.

The difference between a credit union and a commercial bank is that a commercial bank operates for profit where as a credit union does not. What does for profit mean? For profit means that the institution is out to make money off of its clients. Banks are also known for charging higher fees and lower interest rates on their deposit accounts (savings, checking, money market accounts and certificate of deposits). Banks are also controlled by shareholders. Shareholders are persons who have considerable stock within an organization or corporation. This means that the actual clients of a commercial bank have no control over what happens within the institution. Believe it or not there are some positive sides of having an account with a bank. Commercial banks offer convenience along with a wide variety of services such as wealth management, brokerage services, and investments just to name a few. Establishing an account with a bank is a lot easier than establishing an account with a credit union. The commercial bank is open to cliental from the general public, simply anyone can open an account. Unlike credit unions, commercial banks are much larger and have several locations throughout the state or country. Having several locations is convenient to most consumers. Today, consumers like to have everything within reach, including easy access to their funds. Commercial banks are everywhere, as are their automatic teller machines (ATM).

Now that we have the positives and negatives of a commercial bank, let's turn our focus to a credit union. Just like banks, credit unions are financial institutions that offer deposit accounts such as checking and savings accounts. They also offer lending services. However credit unions provide exclusivity. **What does exclusivity mean?** Exclusivity means that establishing an account at a credit union is not open to everyone. You actually have to qualify to become a member. How do you qualify to establish an account with a credit union? The basic qualifications include, but are not limited to the following: having a family member who belongs to a credit union, being an affiliate of a church or organization that belongs to the credit union or being employed with a company or organizations that offer credit union membership to its employees. Unlike commercial banks, credit unions have fewer locations that are not likely connected with other credit unions. This could pose an issue for the average consumer due to lack of convenience. Remember, folks like to have access to their funds. One beneficial difference between a credit union and a commercial bank is that a credit union is controlled by its members. They play a role in what happens within the organization. Another benefit to credit union membership is a low minimum requirement to open an account. This can be as low as $5.00-$10.00.

I can recall when potential clients visited my location. The first thing they would ask was, "Is this a bank?" Although credit unions advertise, they advertise on a smaller scale, and therefore the public is often unaware of their existence and their services. It boils down to public knowledge. My number one job and goal was and is to assist clients in familiarizing themselves with financial basics and addressing their financial needs.

Regardless of whether you choose to join a credit union or a commercial bank, you should make use of as many services as possible. Usually, these services are free. I noticed that clients often wanted to open just a savings account. This would allow them to say they had an affiliation with a financial institution. You are probably asking yourself, is there an issue with having just one savings account? Honestly, there is nothing wrong with having a savings account. This provides a great start to being financially savvy. However, it would benefit you to have a deeper relationship with your institution. A deeper relationship would include having multiple accounts and using the various services that are provided. Again, these services are more than likely free.

So often I would hear statements, such as, "I want to open a checking account but I don't know how it works" or "I have heard several stories with people getting caught up with bouncing checks and accruing fees." After hearing these statements, I was astonished at the fact that many adults did not understand how a basic checking account worked. Although, you may be in this category, you should know that this is NOT uncommon. I had cliental who were doctors and lawyers. These clients had "high" end jobs and didn't know how a basic checking account worked.

Understanding the financial concepts that are spoken in everyday language is the second key to becoming financially successful. Remember, you have to know the basics before advancing to the next level. Let's review key terms that are commonly used. Now before you continue reading, I know that there will be terms that you are familiar with, and you may feel as though you have to bypass this part. I encourage you to skim through this section, because there may be some concepts that may be unclear to you.

There are several types of accounts. As this part of the book series focuses on the basics of finances, we are going to focus on the two main accounts that are often used - savings accounts and checking accounts. Both accounts are used to deposit and withdrawal funds. **The main difference between a savings and checking**

account is that a checking account allows you to write checks. You **cannot** write checks out of a savings account. Yes, it is that simple, nothing more nothing less.

Now that you know the function of a checking account, you should also know that **this is YOUR account** and **it is YOUR responsibility** to review and maintain this account. **It is not the responsibility of the financial institution to maintain this account for you.** I say this so that you understand; you have to take ownership and responsibility for your financial actions. What does it mean to maintain your account? Maintaining your account involves balancing your checkbook. **It is essential that you balance your checkbook on a regular basis. This includes recording every transaction that has been done with this account.** Regular checkbook balancing will be different for each person. This could be every day, every other day, once a week, once every two weeks - you get the point. Getting into the habit of balancing your account will prevent you from overdrawing your account, accumulating overdraft fees and it helps to ensure that your records and the financial institution's records agree. *If and when you are reviewing your statements and feel there is a discrepancy, you have to talk to your institution as soon as possible. Do not wait to get it straightened out. The longer you wait, the harder it will be to fix the issue.* If there are concepts about your checking account that you do not understand or if you are unclear on how to maintain your checking account YOU HAVE TO RESEARCH AND ASK QUESTIONS. Just with anything in life, if you become confused or uncertain about something, you have to ask questions and research until those concepts become clear. The time it takes to master the concept will vary for each person. Keep asking and keep researching until it becomes clear.

Clients often became angry and upset due to issues with their checking account. This is another prime example of the undoubted connection between finances and emotions. Of course, my first goal was to address their emotions and calm them down. I would allow them to rant. After hearing a few minutes (or sometimes more than a few minutes) of crying about fees that they had unknowingly accrued, we could then get down to business. My first question was always, "where is your check register? Let's take a look at it." Often times, my clients would say, "Well I don't keep a register. I keep everything stored in my head." I know that we live in the age of technology. However, until you really get comfortable with knowing the ins and outs of your checking account, please get into the habit of keeping a ledger. They also have smart phone applications that help you keep track of your checking account transactions. Below is a sample of how a check ledger should be kept. If you keep a detailed ledger, I guarantee you; you will not have any trouble. It may seem like a hassle but it will save you time and money in the long run.

As you can see in this example, we started with a balance of $500.00.   We then wrote a check to the eye doctor in the amount of $50.00, leaving our balance at $450.00. When debiting from your checking account, you are simply subtracting an amount from the previous

Check Ledger

Date	Check #	Description	Debit	Credit	Balance	
					$500.00	—Beginning Bal.
1/2/2013	#101	Eye Doctors	$50.00		-$50.00	
					$450.00	— Debit = Subtract
1/7/2013		Payroll Deposit		$700.00	-$700.00	
					$1,150.00	—Credit= Add
1/9/2013		Debit Card for Gas	$40.00		$40.00	
					$1,110.00	
1/10/2013	#102	Phone Bill	$100.00		$100.00	
					$1,010.00	
1/11/2012		ATM Machine	$30.00		$30.00	
		Cash			$980.00	

balance. On January 7th, we received our payroll deposit in the amount of $700.00. This is a credit to our account, therefore we must add the $700.00 to the existing $450.00. This makes our balance $1150.00. Notice that we recorded EVERYTHING in our ledger the checks that we wrote, our payroll deposit, even our ATM withdrawals.

Here is a blank check ledger, use this ledger to start practicing how to record transactions both credits (money placed into the account) and debits (money taken out of the account). Even if you know how to use a ledger but stopped because you were relying on your memory to do your calculations and keep track of credits/debits, you should get back into the habit of using a ledger. It will help you in the long run and is a part of being financially fit. We will start with a balance of $500.00. If you need to, follow the previous example to guide you along.

Check Ledger

Date	Check #	Description	Debit	Credit	Balance
					$500.00

Before we move on, there are a few more concepts that are associated with having a checking account. Let's review the debit card. A debit card actually has two purposes. It serves as an ATM card as well as a credit card. IT IS NOT A CREDIT CARD, the actual funds come out of your checking account. It can be used anywhere you see a Visa® or Master Card® logo. When using this card please log the transaction into your check register. Turn your attention to the previous check ledger example. Notice that when we used our debit card to make a gas purchase, we logged that transaction. Using your debit card is like writing a check; you have to make sure these funds are in the account before you swipe. The next term associated with a checking account is direct deposit. The purpose of direct deposit is to facilitate a convenient and simple way for the depositor (the person/company who is depositing your money), to give you your funds. Usually the funds are available the same day of the deposit. This is more convenient for you. Having an established checking account is important for two reasons: Some employers will only place a direct deposit into a checking account, and most lenders will only debit a checking account for a loan repayment. Having an established checking account also helps you control your spending. By using a check ledger, you can see exactly how you are spending your money.

While working with a financial institution, often times potential clients would come in and attempt to open accounts. I would take their information and process it. I would run their information through "**CHEXSYSTEMS**". What is **CHEXSYSTEMS**? **CHEXSYSTEMS** is a network of financial institutions that share information with one another. These institutions disclose the mishandling of accounts. This information is disclosed by using your social security number. This means, if you are in default (owing money to a financial institution) you will appear on CHEXSYSTEMS. Yes, this issue will follow you until it has been resolved. How long does information stay on file? The information that is listed on **CHEXSYSTEMS** stays on file for five (5) years. If the amount that is owed is paid, it will report as "PAID." If the amount that is owed is unpaid, it will report as "UNPAID." How is the information from **CHEXSYSTEMS** obtained? If in fact you find out that you owe a financial institution, it is your right as a consumer to call **CHEXSYSTEMS** at **(1-800-309-2780)** to find out what financial institution is reporting you for negligent financial behavior. Once you have a listing of what institution(s) has reported you, you then can call the financial institution(s) to make payment arrangements. After attempting to process the information of new clients who were financially negligent, a flag popped up in **CHEXSYSTEMS.** I knew immediately that more than likely the new client was trying to escape a negative financial situation or issue with another institution. They could not open accounts with a new financial institution until the existing situation was resolved.

Electronic Banking

It's 2013 and the world of technology is thriving. Along with the various accounts that financial institutions have, they also offer electronic banking. Electronic banking is nothing more than allowing you to perform banking transactions on the internet through an electronic device, such as a computer, smart phone or tablet. There are a few components to electronic banking which make life really simple, especially for those who are always on the go. These components are: Online statements – which are your paper statements located online. Yes, you can view your statements online. Bill Pay – allows you to pay your bills online. This is usually done thru the institution's website.

Account Ownership

Knowing the various roles that come along with "account ownership" can be a bit confusing. I also noticed that my clients didn't know the difference between a Payable on Death and a Power of Attorney. Along with covering different account terms, it is necessary for us to cover the various aspects of account ownership.

What is account ownership and who can be listed on the accounts? Account ownership is the owner of the account(s). What is the difference between the primary and the joint account holder? The account(s) is listed under the primary account holder's social security number or TIN (Tax ID Number). The joint account holder is listed as a secondary on the account. If the account is joint, both persons can access the account as often as they wish. All parties need not to be present when completing transactions. If the primary account holder dies, the remaining balance of that account goes to the joint owner.* Now that we have discussed the ownership type let us move on to Payable on Death (POD) and Power of Attorney (POA). What is Payable on Death (POD)? A Payable on Death is someone who is listed on the account, other than the primary or joint account owner. This person receives the account balance if the primary or joint owners are deceased. The Payable on Death cannot perform any transactions on this account while either account holder is alive. The order of who receives the account balance if something happens to the primary account holder is as follows:

❖ **Joint Account Owners** – if there is more than one joint owner, then the funds in the account have to be equally split.

Example 1): If John Doe is the primary account holder. He lists Jane Doe, Sally Doe, and Suzie Doe on the accounts as joint owners. Whatever is in the account at the time that Mr. Doe passes is then split equally between Jane, Sally, and Susie.

Example 2): If both John Doe and Jane Doe die, the account balance will be split equally between Jane and Suzie Doe.

❖ **Payable on Death** – If the primary and joint owner(s) both become deceased, the account balance then goes to the payable on death(s). Just like joint owners, the payable on death works the same way.

Example - We already know that John Doe is the primary account holder and has listed Jane, Sally, and Suzie as joint owners. Before John passes away, he has modified the application only listing Jane as the joint owner. However John Sr. has listed Sally, Suzie, and John Doe Jr. as the payable on deaths on all accounts. John Sr. and Jane both have now passed away, which means that the balance is to be split between Sally, Suzie, and John Jr.

Now that we have discussed the Payable on Death – we will now look at the actual role of the Power of Attorney. The role of the Power of Attorney is simple, this Power of Attorney acts on behalf of the actual account holder. Usually this is done for aging parents or relatives who are unable to handle their affairs. In order to facilitate this process, paperwork is completed by the principle (the account holder) who names the actual agent (the power of attorney). Once this process is completed, the paperwork is then reviewed by the financial institution of the principle. The power of attorney ends when the account holder becomes deceased.

*If there are any loans with outstanding balances the funds in the account will be applied to the loan balances.

Seeing What I See

"Try a little harder to be a little better."
— Gordon B. Hinckley – Author

Having been in this industry for over a decade, understanding the different sectors of the financial world has become easy. Am I at a point where I know everything there is to know about finances and money, not at all. I am continuously learning.

With the proper tools and guidance, you can and will begin to see what I see with regards to understanding your financial picture. You will come to a point where understanding finances will become clear. You are probably asking yourself, when will it start to make sense? When will understanding my financial picture become easy? Only you can answer this question. If you continue to read, study and put these financial behaviors that we have and will discuss into practice, over time managing your finances will become second nature.

Before I started working in the financial industry, the financial world was totally complicated. However over time my comfort level with my finances and the finances of my clients became easier. If you are consistent with using the tools we are discussing, you will soon reach this comfort level. It is an ongoing learning process. I am learning something new almost EVERYDAY.

Becoming financially successful goes back to having the mindset of wanting to become better and then doing better. Clients have often mentioned, "This stuff comes so easy to you, how do you do it? You probably can do this with your eyes closed." My response would always be that understanding finances stems from years of training, studying, and practicing. These are the same behaviors and concepts that we are reviewing.

During one of my radio shows, I had a caller who could not understand the principle of not spending money. The caller kept saying over and over, that we are in a culture that manipulates us into spending money. He was convinced that it is a must that we continuously spend money and use credit for everything. My response was simple, "When do we change our thought process? When do we change the culture? When do we get out of the mindset of having to spend money?" The caller responded, "I never thought of it like that, that is a very good point." It's my belief that because people do not understand the nature of not spending money, they feel compelled to spend and rely on credit.

Before you continue reading, I want you to take a moment and ask yourself, why do I spend money? Outside of my necessary expenses, what do I spend money on? How much am I spending daily, weekly, monthly? Take an assessment, of what you spend money on? Be honest with yourself, you will be surprised!

_____

_____

_____

_____

_____

_____

_____

_____

_____

_____

_____

Now that you have taken an assessment of what you actually spend your money on, and how much you are spending, it's now time to see what I see. You do not need to spend as much money as you are spending.

Overcoming Financial Failures

"Listen to the mustn't, child. Listen to the don'ts. Listen to the shouldn'ts, the impossibles, the won'ts. Listen to the never haves, then listen close to me... Anything can happen, child. Anything can be."
— **Shel Silverstein – Author**

It's OK to have fallen but when do you get up, brush your knees off and try again? No one is stopping you from understanding your financial picture but you. Life can and will continue to present you with challenging issues. The key is what you do with those challenges? Do you dwell on those challenges or do you use those challenges as a lesson learned and move on? I hope that you will choose the latter, to learn from those challenges and move on. Overcoming financial failure is just like those challenges of life - you learn from them.

One way to overcome financial failures is to start over. Start from the very beginning. In order to start over you have to first examine what has happened, **what** financial behaviors didn't work, and **why** those behaviors didn't work? Once you have figured the "what" and the "why", you now know **what not to do**.

Why am I broke??

As you continue to travel throughout your financial journey, you probably ask yourself, why the heck am I always broke? Why is it that I never have any money especially after "pay periods"? Honestly, being "broke" is a state of mind and really not an occurrence. If you physically don't have extra money in your pocket, you see yourself as "broke". Before you continue, ask yourself the following questions:

- ❖ Do I have somewhere to sleep regularly?

- ❖ Do I have a means of transportation (whether it be a car or public transportation)?

- ❖ Am I able to eat on a regular basis?

- ❖ Am I able to pay the minimum on my bills? (We will talk about budgeting in chapter 9)

If the answer to these questions is YES, then **YOU ARE NOT BROKE!**

One of my newer clients wanted to meet me so that we can talk about, you guessed it, their finances. They advised me that they wanted to talk about thoroughly understanding their money as they were tired of being broke.   Needless to say, after reviewing my client's financial picture during the initial consultation, we uncovered why my client was failing financially. They were making poor financial decisions along with not keeping track of what was going on with their financial picture.

First thing I informed my client was that they needed to get out of the mindset of spending money. Having the mindset of needing to spend money will result in you physically spending money. I know at times you feel the need to spend extra money that is in your possession or available to you, however you do not need to spend money!!!! Spending money will not complete you! Often after spending time with my clients and figuring out their financial flaws, they usually say, "I just have a spending problem. I have OCD (Obsessive Compulsive Disorder) when it comes to spending money." It is a must that you stop thinking that you need to spend money.

The second thing I informed my client was the need to understand where their money was going monthly. Having an idea of where your money is going every month can prevent you from financial failures. I know that every month you have to pay expenses. Knowing that you have consistent monthly expenses, get into the habit of writing them ALL down.   There are four (4) categories in which you should itemize your expenses.

Here is an example of what your expense chart should look like:

Living Expense	Amount		Operational Expense	Amount
Rent	_____		Gas & Electric	_____
Mortgage	_____		Mobile Phone	_____
Insurance	_____		Insurance (H & L)	_____
Property Tax	_____		Grocery	_____

Transportation Expense	Amount		Miscellaneous Expense	Amount
Car Payment	_____		Entertainment	_____
Car Insurance	_____		Pocket Money	_____
Gas	_____		Personal Care	_____
Car Maintenance	_____			

Let us now go over each category in detail:

Living Expenses - Your living expenses should include rent or mortgage. Your mortgage payment should include an escrow account, which pays your homeowners insurance and your property taxes. Even though these things (property taxes and homeowners insurance) are incorporated into your monthly payment, you should still know what you are paying annually.

Operational Expenses - Your operational expenses should include all routine costs that are needed on a weekly or monthly basis. These expenses would include gas and electric, telephone (mobile or landline), loan repayments, alarm system, grocery, life and health insurance. Your life and health insurances are just as important as your living expenses.

Transportation Expenses – Your transportation expenses should include everything needed for your daily travel. This includes gas. I know that some travel a great distance for work and you may not consider how much this affects your monthly budget. The solution to that is to start tracking your weekly gas expense. Go to the filling station and get gas only - not gum, chips or any of the enticing items that filling stations have. Once you have the amount that it takes to fill up your tank weekly (Sunday – Saturday) multiply this figure times 4 (4 weeks). Doing this will help you realize how much is needed monthly for gas. If you are using public transportation, first consider how often you use public transportation. Doing this will assist you when it comes time to doing your monthly budget. Next, do the pros and cons of getting a weekly metro pass versus getting a monthly metro pass. The monthly metro pass will be more a bit more expensive in the beginning, but it will save you a few bucks over the course of the month. You also have to incorporate car maintenance (oil changes, tire rotation, etc.) into your monthly transportation budget. It is important to comply with your routine maintenance schedule - routine oil changes, tire rotations, and checking fluids.

Miscellaneous Expenses - Your miscellaneous expenses should include entertainment, personal care (hygiene, grooming) and pocket money. Budgeting for emergencies is also important. We will talk about budgeting for emergencies in chapter 9.

Remember the importance of completing your monthly expense chart. This will help you visualize and understand where your money is going.

A New Day

"Isn't it nice to think that tomorrow is a
new day with no mistakes in it yet?"
— **L.M. Montgomery – Author**

It is a new day, with a fresh start. In life we are often given second chances to get it right. Once you realize your past financial mistakes, it's now up to you to take advantage of your fresh start. In the previous chapters we have discussed how to overcome financial failures and the steps to starting over. With a new mindset you have to do just that – start over. Because it's a new day you have to learn how to separate your financial needs from your financial wants. As you start your new journey to becoming financially successful, you have to continuously have conversations with yourself. One thing you need to consider is, if this purchase is necessary or simply desired. Now that you have begun your new financial journey, you have to learn how to curve your financial appetite. You can no longer allow your wants or desires to get you into financial trouble.

So often we want to be like others and have those things that we know that we cannot afford, - a new house, a new car, or even a new pair of shoes. We like to call this "keeping up with the Jones"". No longer must you feel compelled to keep up with others, this causes you to live beyond your means. You can no longer worry about what others say or feel if you don't have a "certain look". By trying to maintain an unrealistic lifestyle, you financially bite off more than you can handle.

As a financial consultant I notice that there are always clients who have the latest fashions and cash in their pockets. However, those same clients who appear as if they have everything in place often have accounts that stay overdrawn. Not only does this reflect mismanagement of finances, it also reflects misplaced priorities.

Before you continue, ask yourself why do you feel compelled to keep up with others? BE HONEST WITH YOURSELF. Once you have answered this question, take a few minutes and list ways to change this mindset.

_____

_____

_____

_____

_____

_____

_____

_____

Another mindset that you have to change is caring what others think. Oftentimes the reason that you feel compelled to keep up with others is because you give great consideration to what others think about you. Wait! I am not saying that you should stay isolated and disconnected from others, but you should not allow the thoughts of others to control your spending.

As a teller, I can remember a client, who if you looked at him you would think he was actually poor. He wore a pocketed shirt with pen stains. He wore the same brown slacks, and he wore the same pair of worn shoes. Not only did he look rugged, he drove a yellow 4 door Pinto. Every time he came up to the counter to do a transaction, I was amazed at the balances he had in **_ALL_** of his accounts. Yes this client had several certificates of deposits (CD's) and money manager accounts. The total balance in his accounts was a little over $650,000.00. In knowing client's balance, it was evident that he could have taken himself on a shopping spree, and bought a few expensive cars. He chose to save his money and did not give consideration to what others thought or said about his appearance. WOW! My peers at work would always ask him, why he didn't go shopping to get new clothes, or at least get a new car. His response was simply," I have nothing to prove to anyone. I go to work, do my job and go home." After hearing this, I sat in amazement; I actually liked this client's attitude towards his appearance and life in general. In looking at his outer appearance, you would think he was broke, but it was the complete opposite.

We also need to learn to live beneath our means. Living beneath your means is simply not spending every dollar that you have in your possession or available to you. Look at the client who had $650,000.00 in his accounts, how he was dressed and what he drove. That is a prime example of living under your means. Remember that in order to take advantage of this second chance you have to adjust your mindset. Start with recognizing if your purchases are needs or wants, refrain from giving a lot of consideration to what others think about your lifestyle and always live beneath your means.

The "I Can Do This" Attitude

"Success is not final, failure is not fatal:
it is the courage to continue that counts."
— Winston Churchill — Author

The reoccurring theme throughout this series is and will continue to be to change your mindset. You have to come to a place where you want to become better and start taking the steps to do better, this takes will power. In order to have the mindset of becoming financially successful you first have to understand your financial picture and how it works. In previous chapters we discussed the aspects of knowing and how to start understanding your finances; it is now time to put what you have learned into practice.

Understanding your finances is just like understanding life. After figuring out your financial mistakes, you now have to have the **"I CAN DO THIS"** attitude. The **"I CAN DO THIS"** attitude is a self-explanatory mindset that you can apply to every area of your life. With this attitude, you can and will overcome any obstacle that presents itself, **including your finances**.

I recently had a conversation with a business owner. She informed me that she was on the brink of shutting down her business. After asking why, she informed me that she was tired of all of the mishaps and challenges of the business. People were not doing what they had promised. While having this conversation, she expressed that she literally had to do everything except sell her soul to keep the business running. I could hear the tiredness and frustration in her voice. After letting her vent, I then said to her. "Life will present us challenges and issues. Sometimes those issues and challenges that are presented will try to break us. It is up to us to stand strong and have the mindset that we can make it work". I could sense the tiredness and the breaking point where she and many of you are headed. What I suggest that you do is step back, let yourself breathe mentally, physically, and emotionally. In stepping back, allow yourself to revamp and figure out what it is that you want to do. Once you have taken the time to regroup, come back with a clear head, and give it your all.

In having the "**I CAN DO THIS**" attitude with your finances, you should not look at this as a tedious process. Believe it or not you can have fun with it. You literally have to have fun with it. If not you will drive yourself insane!

My clients have come to appreciate the concepts that I teach, such as the "$30.00 diet" and the "I don't have it" approach. I have several clients now that are quick to say, "My financial coach says I don't have it, and I really don't have it." Every time I hear this, I am reassured that they are learning, understanding and applying the concepts that are being taught.

People don't realize that they have spent too much money until it's too late. After noticing the continuation of people spending too much money, having nothing to show for it, and performing several budget analyses, I formulated a plan. What I do with this plan is an allocation of money for all expenses, as we discussed previously - living, transportation, operational, and miscellaneous. Once the allocations have been done, I then see what the client has left over. Regardless of how much money is available, I allot the client $30.00 for two weeks. They are not allowed to spend more than $30.00. The goal of this exercise is to demonstrate that if you are aware of your spending and really consider your wants versus your needs, you can curve your unnecessary spending habits. Folks actually laugh when I inform them that they will be on a cash spending diet. Often times I receive the same reaction which is "$30.00 is no money - that is impossible." They often think it is impossible, until they try it. Most of them have succeeded with this task and have come to realize that although it is challenging, it is doable and fun.

I can recall a client who developed the **"I CAN DO THIS"** attitude when she was placed on the $30.00 diet. Once the initial shock wore off she felt liberated. By our fourth session, she realized her success and exclaimed, "It works, the $30.00 diet really works." For the two weeks she didn't have to spend money, because she ate breakfast at home in the morning, and she packed her lunch every day. During our time together my client then informed me that she was able to put extra money on expenses which could have never been done before.

I share that story with you so that you can start to change your way of thinking. Let's say for instance that my client was hesitant on trying the $30.00 diet, she would have probably kept spinning her financial wheels going nowhere and continuing to get the same empty results. However, because she was willing to try something new, what happened, - her mindset was changed and she received different results.

Another approach to the **"I CAN DO THIS"** attitude is repeating the **"I don't have it"** phrase to yourself. The "I don't have it" approach is also self-explanatory. With this approach you tell yourself that you don't have extra money to spend frivolously. Believe it or not, it's often times the truth.

Many clients tell me that, they have become experts at window shopping. Who doesn't window shop? Believe me, there is a huge difference in window shopping with an understanding that you cannot physically purchase anything; in comparison to window shopping, making unplanned purchases and worrying about the aftermath

later.   Before beginning the Understanding Finances
Program, my clients often inform me that they practiced
impulse spending; which is an unhealthy financial behavior.   However, after working through the program, they
now understand that it is not financially healthy to spend
money, just because it is there to spend.

Making a whole lot out of a little is another approach that is helpful as you continue towards your quest
for financial success.   Making a whole lot out of a little
simply means that you are making the best out of what
you have.   You come to realize what *is* important versus
what *is not* important.   The same client that was willing
to try the $30.00 diet had an annual income that was a
little above $32,000. Today, $32,000 is not a lot of money
for a family of four.   However she now understands that
while her income may not be a lot, she has the tools to
make the best of her situation.   You may not have
everything that you **desire**, when it comes to money.
However, count it all joy because your basic financial
needs are being met.   Learn how to look at the glass as
half full, instead of half empty.

The Reality of Saving Money

"The way to get started is to quit talking and begin doing."
— **Walt Disney**

You now know that it's a new day and that you now have the mindset of saving money. The fact of the matter is that you have to DO IT. You have to get into the habit of saving money. You are probably saying to yourself, I can't save money or I don't have any money to save. In the previous chapters we discussed the notion of having the "I Can Do It" attitude. It is here and now that you apply this attitude. You have to have the **inner strength** and the **willingness** to want to save money and <u>then start saving.</u>

Often times I speak with young people, it seems like they have everything, from IPhones® to IPads® and everything in between. As parents is it a must that we run and purchase the latest gadget or toy for our child(ren)? What are we really teaching our children? We have all heard the concept of "saving for a rainy day". As mentioned earlier, I gave that same speech to my clients when I was a bank teller. Why is saving money in so hard? Is it because people don't have money to save, or is it that we think tomorrow will take care of itself? When performing initial consultations, one consistent long term goal that my clients have is to save at least $500-$1000 by the next calendar year. You may say saving $500.00 is easy; I can do that in a matter of months. While this may seem easy for some, for others the notion of saving money is extremely hard.

Why save money? What's the point, I can't take it with me when I die. Sound familiar? You are absolutely correct; you cannot take your money with you when you pass away. Why continue to practice poor financial behaviors while you are still alive? What are you teaching your children or others who may look up to you? What financial legacy are you leaving for the next generation? We already discussed why it is essential that you understand your financial picture. It is now time for us to discuss the aspects of budgeting and to understand why this is important, and an essential key step on your financial journey. A budget is nothing more than a plan of how much money is needed for your expenses. Why is budgeting important? Budgeting is important because it sets a solid foundation of every financial plan.

You are probably asking yourself, how do I start a budget, where do I begin? Starting a budget requires you to know two things - what expenses are to be paid and what dollar amount should be paid to those expenses. (Review the expense chart that we created in the "Overcoming Financial Failures" section). Knowing what expenses need to be paid regularly can be a bit confusing because there are two types of expenses – necessary expenses and unnecessary expenses. A necessary expense is classified as an essential expense that needs to be paid regularly. As mentioned before, there are 4 categories of necessary expenses which include (living expenses, operational expenses, transportation expenses, and miscellaneous expenses).

Now that we have clarified what a necessary expense is, let's briefly discuss the meaning of an unnecessary expense. So often you see yourself, as being "broke". As mentioned before, being broke is a mindset and it also comes from practicing unhealthy financial behaviors. Spending money on unnecessary expenses is a huge part of practicing poor financial behaviors. Examples of unnecessary expenses include but are not limited to: eating out, purchasing an item that you cannot afford, lending money to others and excessive entertainment expenses.

I recently had a conversation with a client who advised me that they really need to go on a financial diet. This person spends $159.00 a week on food (eating out). Let's do a simple calculation. Multiply $159 x 52 weeks in a year. That is a total of $8268.00 that this client spends on a eating out a year!

Let's review how much the average American spends on dining out. This scenario is done for 5 days out of the week for one individual (without family).

> **Breakfast:** A cup of fancy coffee from a coffee house or a breakfast sandwich - $5.00

> **Lunch:** A salad or soup and sandwich with a drink - $10.00

> **Dinner:** Sub, fries, and a large drink or a large one topping pizza $10.00

**$25.00 x 5 (days a week) x 52 (weeks in a year) = <u>$6500.00</u>

Based on our scenario, the average American spends $6500.00 annually on eating out. *That is a lot of money.* For someone with a yearly income of $33,600.00 who spends $6500.00 on dining out. Dining out consumes 19% of their income. **The average food expense should be no more than 11-12% of your annual budget.**

Life will throw us financial curve balls. If or when those curve balls arise, will you be prepared? These curve balls are called emergencies. In the "Overcoming Financial Failures" section, I mentioned having your car serviced on a regular basis. Have you noticed that almost every time you go to get routine maintenance for your vehicle, when the service tech comes to you with a clip board in hand, you know that you are about to spend some major money.

A client called me over the summer, and needed rotors for her car. The first thing she did before making a decision was to give me a call. This signified that even for an emergency or an unforeseen expense, she was THINKING about her spending. The client said, "Robin, I am at the mechanic, and I need rotors for my car, I don't have any money to get this done, can I use my credit card?" My response was yes, you need rotors for your car so use your credit card. However let's formulate a game plan to pay this balance off in thirty (30) business days.

Not that you are wishing that an emergency will happen but you should get in to the habit of planning for an emergency. Getting into the habit of planning for an emergency will eliminate an emotional breakdown when the emergency occurs and emergencies will occur.

Out of sight out of mind – Learn how to set up an account at another financial institution. This account should not be located where you house your primary accounts.

A few of my clients mentioned that once they have a complete understanding of their finances, they wanted to establish an account as a savings tool. I suggested they open an account with ING®. Not only will the money be out of site and out of mind. It will also be extremely hard to get.

Planning for the future – Another reason why you should save is to plan for the future. I like to call this, the now versus the later concept. Planning for the future simply means you need to establish some type of retirement account, whether it be a 401K (an employee sponsored plan) or an IRA (Individual Retirement Account, which is usually housed at a financial institution).

Thinking about attending college or sending you child(ren) to college? This is another reason why you should plan to save money. The average annual cost for tuition, fees, room & board and books at a four (4) year college in-state is estimated at $18,928.00. If you are thinking of venturing to another state or a private college, this could be considerably more.

Saving for fun - Want to take yourself on a shopping spree in the near future? Why not plan to save for shopping. We talked about saving for emergencies and a rainy day. You can also save for a fun event like shopping or a vacation. Remember, you have to learn how to have fun while understanding your finances.

The Continuous Journey of Becoming and Staying Financially Successful

"If you can't fly then run, if you can't run then walk, if you
can't walk then crawl, but whatever you
do you have to keep moving forward."
— **Martin Luther King Jr.**

Now that you have the right tools and you know that it takes preparation to become financially successful, it is time to start setting attainable goals for yourself. Setting goals that you can achieve will allow you to feel some sort of accomplishment. Having a game plan to assist you in reaching your financial goals provides a visual outline for what needs to be done in order to reach these goals. Your goal structure should be outlined as follows:

• **Annually**: What is it that you want to have accomplished financially by this time next year? Set a twelve month, long term financial goal.

❖ Example: I will save $1200 over the next 12 months.

- **Quarterly**: Realize that there are 4 quarters in a year. For each quarter, set at least 2 specific and realistic goals.

  - ❖ Example: I plan to save $300 during the first quarter of the year.

  - ❖ Example: I plan to pay off half of one credit card during the second quarter of this year.

- **Monthly**: There are 3 months in every quarter. Each month, you should set one or two smaller but realistic goals. Although these goals are smaller, they will still help you to accomplish your larger goals – quarterly/annual/lifetime financial goal.

  - ❖ Example: I plan to pay an extra $30.00 per pay period towards one credit card balance.

  - ❖ Example: I will place myself on a $30.00 cash only, spending diet for the month of January.

Notice that for each example provided, the goals are specific, realistic and time sensitive. If your goals are vague, unrealistic or are not associated with a specified time frame, you are not likely to accomplish the goal(s).

Goal Allocation:

Before you continue reading what are some financial goals that you would like to achieve?

Annually: _____

_____

_____

Quarterly: _____

_____

_____

Monthly: _____

_____

_____

Regularly reassessing your financial goals is important. Also, considering more than one way to accomplish your goals is always helpful. If you notice that one way is not working, you should consider another way to accomplish your goals. When counseling my clients, I always inform them that they should have at least three ways to obtain the same solution. This is to ensure that if plan A and B does not work, then they have a plan C.

Staying focused and determined are the last key steps on your financial path. Once you apply the "I Can Do It" attitude, you have to use your inner strength to keep this momentum going. Please do not think that everything will be smooth sailing. Getting a better understanding of your finances, as well as changing your financial behaviors is a big step. With understanding, patience and endurance, you are on your way to financial success!

Your Financial Ladder

"Kites rise highest against the wind, not with it."
— Winston S. Churchill – Author

Here is a ladder of your new financial path. First and for most you must **understand** your finances. With having a complete understanding you then can start to **prepare** yourself, spiritually, mentally, emotionally and physically. The third step in your financial path is having a **mindset** to become financially successful. As we mentioned earlier, your actions will follow your mind. Now that you have changed your mindset it is now time to start planning for the future. This requires setting attainable **goals**. Once these goals are in place, create a budget. **Budgeting** helps you visualize what needs to be done to reach your goals. Lastly, as you continue on your financial path, have the **determination** to do better with achieving financial success. Put the "I Can Do It" attitude into practice. Having this attitude will comfort and help you as you travel towards financial greatness. At times you may want to stop climbing, give up, or throw in the towel. I encourage you to continue to climb. The reward will be much greater once you get to the top.

Wrap Up

"Our greatest glory is not in never falling,
but in rising every time we fall."
— **Confucius**

Congratulations! You have finished this part of the series. It is my hope and desire that your fear of finances has lessened and that you are now able to see your finances in a clearer light. I encourage you to continue to use the tools that have been provided. In addition, do not forget to use the thoughts and ideas that you have written throughout this book. These will serve as a guide as you travel along your financial journey. Considering what financial institution best fits your financial needs, understanding the financial concepts and terms that are used daily, learning why budgeting is important, along with knowing how to write and prepare for your financial goals are keys to becoming financially successful. To build on this foundation future books of this series will cover the following topics: *the importance of credit* and *retirement.* Before we close, let's revisit the financial questions that you were asked at the very beginning. Hopefully you now have the key elements to becoming financially successful and you will answer these questions differently.

What are your strongest financial areas?

_____

_____

What are your weakest financial areas?

_____

_____

What do you fear the most about finances?

_____

_____

Frequently Asked
Banking Questions

Below is a list of frequently asked banking questions **(FAQs)**

<u>Savings Account FAQs</u>

What are the fees associated with a savings account?
Fees may vary based upon the institution. When establishing your account, please consult with your financial institution. It is best to do the research prior to you visiting the institution.

Do I need a specific amount of money to establish a savings account? Prior to opening your savings account, please consult with your financial institution as the opening amounts will vary.

How do I withdraw my money out of this account?
You will need to visit the institution where your funds were deposited, and advise the teller that you want to make a withdrawal. You can also request an ATM (Automatic Teller Machine) card at the time of establishing your account. This will enable you to withdraw money from the ATM.

What's an Automatic Teller Machine? This is a machine that houses money. When your financial institution is closed, you simply go the ATM machine, insert the card, key in your secret PIN (personal identification number) and there you have it -YOUR CASH. You may need to make a withdraw from an ATM that is not affiliated with your banking institution. There may be fees charged by the bank that owns the ATM. There may also be a fee from your bank for utilizing another bank's ATM. Be aware that ATM fees can chip away at the money that you have saved.

Checking account FAQ

Do I need a specific amount of money to establish a checking account? Prior to opening your checking account, please consult with your financial institution as these fees will vary.

Electronic Banking FAQs

How can I access electronic banking on my computer? Once your accounts have been established simply inform your financial institution that you are interested in electronic (online) banking. The bank will provide you with the website, a temporary login and password. Once this information is provided, the account holder visits the website and is often prompted to create a new login and password.   The features of on-line banking vary by institution.

Can I pay my bills on-line through my bank? Can my financial institution enable a particular bill to be paid every month at the same time? The answer to both of these questions is yes. Most institutions offer on-line bill pay. You can set your bill payment up for reoccurring payments. This will enable your bills to be paid the same time each month. If for some reason, you decide that you want to stop the reoccurring payments, simply go into the bank and request to stop the automatic payment or make the adjustment on-line. If you discontinue automatic bill payment, you will have to log in every month to pay that bill.

What if I want to receive my banking statements online and in the mail, can I have both? This honestly depends on the financial institution.   Most institutions allow for one or the other but not both. There is a big push to do everything electronically, thus phasing out paper statements.

What is mobile banking? Mobile banking is a method of electronic banking that can be done by either your smart phone, or your tablet. I like to call it ***banking on***

the go. With mobile banking you can do the exact same thing on your smart phone that you can do on your computer.

Client Testimonials

R. West – Washington, DC

"Mrs. Haynes has been my first and only financial coach. Before coming to her I was lost in the financial spectrum. I was in my junior year of college not really making money, with no established credit and was looking to build on my finances. I had been with my financial institution for about 4 years prior to meeting Mrs. Haynes. She has taught me the importance of having good credit and knowing how to manage my finances. Since meeting her I am have become financially sound. She is the best financial coach, and a true friend!"

M. Milledge – Baltimore, MD

"I thought I was managing my money in a good way by telling myself that I had good money management skills. To my surprise that was untrue! I set a goal for myself to buy a house but I knew my credit and ability to save money wasn't good. So I reached out to Robin who was recommended to me by a mutual friend. Robin and I met and it was during the meeting that she created a budget for me to follow. She counseled me and made me understand the importance of making a budget work for me so I could continue to add to my birds nest instead of taking away from it. Since I have been following the budget plan I can proudly say that I have improved my credit score and I am currently in the process of buying my first home. Thanks Robin for your expertise and honesty."

T. Cornish – Baltimore, MD

"Before I met Robin I was really depressed over my finances; I tried many times to sit down and develop a budget on my own; however I failed EVERYTIME!! Robin taught me discipline, which allowed me to see that I was wasting too much money on frivolous things and not putting enough on my important bills. I also learned that I was in a cycle of spending out of frustration because I felt that there was not enough money to cover my expenses and have spending money. However, Robin taught me a method that allows me to pay my bills ON TIME as well as have spending money. I can honestly say that Understanding Finances has been a blessing to me and without thier expertise I would have continued to travel on a road of debt!!"

N. Owens – Severn, MD

"Robin has helped me manage and save my money so that I could purchase a car. She showed me how I could save a few dollars every time I get paid and put myself on a budget. After doing so for a few months I had enough money for a nice size down payment for my car. I still save and budget my money and I haven't missed a car payment yet. Thank you Robin"

Connect With Robin

Visit Robin on the web at
www.understandingfinances.org

You can also follow her online at
www.facebook.com/Robin R. Haynes
www.twitter.com/Knowing_Money

Interested in having Robin speak to your church,
organization, or school?
Email her at info@understandingfinances.org

CPSIA information can be obtained at www.ICGtesting.com
Printed in the USA
BVOW010105200213

313642BV00004B/1/P